THE WORLD'S BEST COLLECTION OF PUNS

Says a guy on the internet

First published in the United Kingdom 2020.

Copyright © Daily Dafty
Publication by © Plan4 Media
© Mairi

A catalogue record of this book is available from
the British Library.

ISBN: 978-1-907463-87-7

For Mairi, chief editor at the Daily Dafty for her groundbreaking puns. For her hard work and dedication every day—without complaint—and for her drive and energy to make sure the readers are supplied with fresh daily content every single day—without fail.

Without you, there would be less laughter in the world—and less love.

To Connor & Liam

Puns are one of the most common everyday forms of humour, and are often thought of and dispatched from the school playground all the way through to the workplace and onto the internet.

Puns are regarded as forms of wordplay that can consist of double to multiple meanings. They can be smart, silly, and even deserve an instant eye roll.

It is said some of the world's first puns were written in ancient times as far back as the Romans.

Enjoy this fine collection of some of the world's best puns *(according to a guy on the internet).*

My grandmother used to give
me pocket money if I sang ABBA
songs for her.
I loved to sing for Nan dough.

My wife had an accident with a
needle and thread.
The doctor said she was lucky to
pull through.

The worst pub I ever drank in was
called 'The Fiddle'.
It really was a vile inn.

My wife was accused of stealing a poppy, but the police had to let her go because they couldn't pin it on her.

My grandfather died after being hit by a tennis ball.
My long-suffering grandmother said at the funeral: "It was a lovely service."

When I was working as a porter in a hospital, I got sacked due to alleged bullying claims.
I was accused of pushing people around.

My girlfriend left me due to my addiction to horse racing.
I knew it wouldn't last furlong.

My neighbour was telling me he got arrested for blasting out Engelbert Humperdinck songs late at night.
He told me: "Police released me... let me go."

I painted half my face like a clown then drove around town.
I'm not sure everyone saw the funny side, though.

Beyoncé was spotted at our local supermarket.
She was with Aldi single ladies.

I knew a man who couldn't stop singing Frank Sinatra and Dean Martin songs.
He's just been diagnosed with crooner virus.

John Travolta's pepper farm is going from strength to strength according to his latest set of accounts.
He said: "I've got chillies; they're multiplying."

I went to the doctor to get help with my Sinead O'Connor obsession.
Guess what he told me?
Guess what he told me?

I bought my girlfriend some glow-in-the-dark makeup.
You should have seen her face light up.

My dad was shot 200 times with an upholstery gun.
Fortunately, he is now fully recovered.

A British man was quarantined after he was caught importing a large collection of autos from China.
It appears he has caught the car owner virus.

I am thinking of buying a greyhound, but I'm not sure what the wife will say.
I think I'll run it by her first.

My mate has stunned the fuel industry after discovering petrol made from insect urine.
I think it's BP.

A violent storm has destroyed Cat Steven's caravan.
I heard him singing, 'My awning has broken.'

I regret dating two psychiatrists at the same time. The hangovers are hellish.
You should never mix your shrinks.

A man was rushed to hospital after complaining of Irish voices rumbling in his belly.
It looks like he's suffering from a stomach Ulster.

A Blackpool donkey is in a critical condition after eating a window.
That's a pane in the ass.

Barry Gibb used to love working in Chinese restaurants before he found fame.
He said: "Well, you can tell by the way I use my wok."

I returned home to find all my carpets and mats have been stolen.
I think it is the work of rug addicts.

My brother and I inherited furniture from the local zoo. I'm happy to say I got the lion's chair.

A woman has given birth to identical twins named Juan and Amal.
She said: "I only carry one photograph because when you've seen Juan, you've seen Amal."

A Russian acrobat who was part of a pyramid scheme has been deported. Now we don't have Oleg to stand on.

A monk who saw the face of Jesus in his margarine tub couldn't believe it wasn't Buddha.

I gave my girlfriend a medieval battle uniform to polish while I went to the pub.
She always wanted a night in shining armour.

A mobster is to combine his taxidermy business with bomb-making.
He said: "I'm going to make you an otter you can't defuse."

I was kicked out of the cookery
class for using a giant spoon.
It seems I caused quite a stir.

I was thrown out of my local pet
shop for lining up gerbils in order
of height.
They didn't like me critter sizing.

I bought a giraffe on Amazon.
I am doubtful it will be delivered
on time. It's a tall order.

My mum was crying because she'd run out of fabric softener.
I managed to offer her a small amount of comfort.

A boy who skipped school to go bungee jumping is suspended.

I can't recall working in the pencil rubber factory.
It seems my memory has been erased.

My friend has an urge to paint
herself gold.
It sounds like she has a gilt
complex.

I got a job in a prison brothel.
It's not the best job in the world,
but it has its pros and cons.

My plastic surgeon was sacked for
using helium instead of silicone.
It all went tits up.

Wild West outlaw liked to squirt
ink in his spare time.
'Billy the Squid'.

A T.V. weatherman broke both
arms and legs.
He had to call from his hospital
bed to tell us about his four casts.

My girlfriend dumped me because
of my obsession with plants.
I said: "Where's this stemming
from, petal?"

A dog walker was attacked by a herd of sheep.
Fortunately, he was only grazed.

A tall man was hospitalized after banging his head on a low bridge.
He said: "I would've been okay if viaduct."

I'm off work because my pet cow is sick.
My boss thinks I'm milking it.

I shared a taxi with some spotty youths.
I think it was an acne carriage.

I saw a movie about a guy who experiences amazing revelations while eating cereal.
'Breakfast Epiphanies'.

I used to work as a lumberjack, but I couldn't hack it, so they gave me the axe.

Never date a telecoms engineer.
He has too many hang-ups.

A limbo dancer married the local
locksmith.
The wedding was very low key.

A thug who assaulted a man with
a measuring tape battered him to
within an inch of his life.

I became ill after eating too many
snooker balls.
The doctor said I wasn't getting
enough greens.

I was nervous about having to
talk to strangers on a cruise I was
about to embark on.
My friend told me: "Don't worry,
we're all in the same boat."

Native American who drank 10
gallons of Darjeeling was found
dead in his tea-pee.

A thief has been arrested after stealing the big clock from the centre court at Wimbledon.
He's currently serving time.

A sick grizzly bear isolated himself in the wild during the coronavirus outbreak.
He's not out of the woods yet.

The 'Irritable Bowel Society' is to present a version of 'The Sound of Music' for its members.
It's called 'How Do You Solve a Problem Like My Rear?'

A drifter who stole perfume and aftershave from a department store was charged with fragrancy.

A chatterbox woman was slammed by animal rights activists for talking the hind legs off a donkey.

A scriptwriter pours Bisto into graves.
He wanted to see the plot thicken.

An ice-cream van was robbed.
Police have coned off the area.

North Pole bear refuses to mate
with South Pole penguin.
It seems they are polar opposites.

A woman dressed as a jigsaw
puzzle left a fancy dress party
early.
She said she didn't fit in.

I met the wife at a Bring & Buy sale.
She said it was fête, but I thought it was a little bazaar.

Man splits with his archaeologist wife after accusing her of always digging up the past.

I headed off on a spiritual journey wearing camouflage clothing in a bid to find myself.

I took a budget airline to court
after my luggage went missing.
I lost my case.

A lorry carrying strawberries
overturns on the motorway.
It caused a jam.

Burglars stole all my anti-
depressants.
I hope they are happy now.

A lorry carrying wigs overturns on the motorway.
Police are combing the area.

I took a double-glazing company to court over shoddy workmanship.
I was awarded condensation.

I was shocked to find out my vibrator was worth a lot of money.
All this time I've been sitting on a small fortune.

I was falsely accused of stealing salt from my local supermarket.
I was visibly shaken.

My friend suggested we go to our next fancy dress party as a grouse and a pheasant.
I told her: "I'm game if she is."

A woman who divorced her cosmetic surgeon after he cheated on her said: "Thanks for the mammaries."

I watched a compelling documentary about sniffing adhesives.
I was glued to the screen.

80s rock legend has fallen on hard times.
'Cindi Pauper'.

I used to work in a vegetable processing factory until I was caught taking a pea.

A man who had head removal
surgery said: "That's
a weight off my shoulders."

Power failure at Bruce Springsteen
concert.
Fans were left dancing in the dark.

I was sectioned for destroying all
my mint-flavoured cigarettes in a
fit of rage.
The doctor said I had suffered a
menthol breakdown.

Disney movie slammed for too
much swearing.
Movie bosses revealed '101
Damnations' has been axed.

A man who quit his job as a butler
in a stately home said: "I didn't
like being ordered around
in that manor."

I complained to a music store
that I couldn't find any CDs by
Aerosmith and Run-DMC.
I was told, "Walk This Way."

A locksmith was promoted.
He said: "Knowing how to pick
locks has opened up a lot of doors
for me."

Channel 4 has announced a new
show where farmers go to each
other's harvest and secretly
rate them. It's called "Combine
With Me."

A baker who was famous for his
donuts has closed his shop after
50-years.
He said he just got sick of the hole
thing.

A transvestite has escaped from police custody.
Officers fear he may be a broad.

A daytime T.V. show discovers Joe Strummer's skeleton in the loft of a house.
As a mark of respect, 'Clash in the Attic' has been axed.

An overweight alcoholic transvestite said: "All I ever wanted to do was eat, drink, and be Mary."

A dog breeder's bulldog gave birth to a litter of Shih Tzus but then complained that nobody was buying his bullshit.

I phoned the Samaritans because I was going to throw myself under a train.
They told me to stay on the line.

When I first held a universal remote control in my hand, I thought, wow, this changes everything.

A blind couple who split after a few weeks said: "We just couldn't see eye-to-eye."

When I was in prison, the guards taught me proper grammar and punctuation.
They said it would help to reduce my sentence.

My neighbour couldn't afford to pay her water bill.
She was sent a 'get well' card.

I lost my job as a graffiti artist.
To be fair, the writing was on the
wall for a while.

I never realized that I married a
communist.
I guess I should have seen all the
red flags.

I was paranoid after seeing some
Peruvian owls spying on me.
I'm sure they were Inca hoots.

The local wig shop was broken into.
Police confirmed all locks had to be replaced.

My daughter's new boyfriend accidentally trod on my freshly-laid cement.
He didn't leave a good impression.

I realized I am not a fan of lemon preserve after all these years.
It just a curd to me.

When I worked as a baggage handler, I would smear all the luggage handles with Vaseline. I got away with it because the police kept dropping the case.

My uncle was crushed by a piano. His funeral was very low key.

My dad ordered A4 laser print paper online, but he received cardboard instead. He wrote the company a stiff letter.

My wife went to a posh party where all the ladies were knitting and drinking.
She had Pimm's and needles.

I love to keep my tropical fish at home in a tank.
It has a calming effect on my brain — it must be all the indoor fins.

Sting has launched a new aromatherapy range.
It's a massage in a bottle.

At the party, people were giving
each other bits of ravioli.
They were playing pasta parcel.

I asked our librarian if she knew of
any authors who wrote dinosaur
books.
She told me: "Try Sarah Topps."

A handsome tramp was caught
hanging around a pub chatting up
a girl.
Dirty bar stud!

I hate horse chestnut trees, but I hope to conker my fear.

I saw Mike Jagger in Tesco panic buying toilet paper and a pumice stone.
I know it's only rock 'n roll, but I like it.

I divorced my wife because she was addicted to counting.
I wonder what she's up to now.

A T.V. weatherman turned nasty
after he was sacked for giving
too many hazy and frosty
forecasts.
No more mist and ice guy.

I love doing stand-up comedy at
the fertility clinic.
I always get a standing ovulation.

The local cheesemaker has finished
painting his second-hand, rusty,
old boat.
He double Gloucester.

I saw a man painting pictures of bicycles on the local church roof. I think it was cycle Angelo.

Toy Story's Woody was forced to quit playing his guitar. He said: "I don't know where my Pixar."

There were no ATMs around at the time of the dinosaurs. They had to use Tyrannosaurus cheques.

A pair of jeans took a belt to court over 'support issues'.
The jeans lost the case because the belt found a loophole.

My American friend planned to save pound coins and put them in a jar. I said: "Where's the cents in that?"

A thief stole my spectacles.
I will find him; I have contacts.

A troublemaker wearing a tie fastener caused mayhem in our local pub. The landlord told him: "We don't like your tie pin here."

My mate got engaged to a pencil. He's looking forward to introducing all his friends to his bride 2B.

Army horticulturist failed to show up at his barracks.
He went absent without leaf.

One year on since the passing of Peter Tork from The Monkees; his fans have joined together to sing 'I'm a beriever'.

My wife was killed in a rollerblading accident after buying a pair from Poundland. She always was a cheapskate.

Police are hunting for a mugger who threatens his victim with a lighted match. They want to capture him before he strikes again.

My friend caught coronavirus
whilst on holiday in Paris.
She told me: "Now Eiffel sick."

My son was up all night answering
questions on resistors and
conductors.
His teacher always sets too much
ohm work.

I'm coming to the end of a 24-hour
trouser pressing competition.
I'm on my last leg now.

My son broke his PlayStation.
I couldn't console him.

I cheated on the woman who is the voice of the speaking clock.
Now she won't give me the time of day.

I'll never forget my second marriage.
It was a wife-changing experience.

I was in tears after I botched my interview for the job in the scissor factory.
They said I didn't make the cut.

A British man was hospitalised in Moscow after being stung by a dodgy-looking wasp while visiting the Kremlin.
I suspect it was the cagey bee.

I was arrested after I crashed my car to avoid hitting a stray octopus.
The police released me because they couldn't find any squid marks.

A fraudster who installed kitchen worktops for a living is jailed.
It seems he was arrested for counter fitting.

I saw a giant lizard sitting on a portable toilet at the local zoo.
I think it was a commode-o-dragon.

I am addicted to eating sofas.
I have a suite tooth.

A man with a rare shrinking disease is warned by his doctor: "You'll just have to be a little patient."

My Irish wife left me after 35-years of marriage because I was obsessed with 80s music.
I said to her: "Oh, come on, Eileen."

My friend Bilbo has trouble with self-checkouts in Tesco. It keeps telling him there's an unexpected item in the Baggins area.

I started up a successful business building yachts in my attic.
Sails are going through the roof.

I went swimming in the sea and was disgusted when a fish crapped on me.
It was a little bass turd.

A pharmaceutical company has announced the launch of an expensive laxative.
Compared to cheaper varieties, this one will certainly give you a run for your money.

Our farmhand was assaulted and kicked in the crotch. He sued his employer for all his land. Unfortunately, he only ended up with a couple of achers.

I accidentally inserted my 'Iceland' card into the ATM instead of my bank card.
My account was frozen.

There was utter chaos after new bamboo trees were planted at the local zoo.
It was pandamonium out there.

I just ate the 'recently deceased'
section of my newspaper.
It was a bit chewy.

My ex-wife took me to court about
a dispute over who owned our
apple pies.
She got custardy.

A man who identifies fungus for a
living quits out of boredom.
He said: "Every day, it's just the
same mould, same mould."

My husband, who works at Kwik Fit, has confessed to throwing balls at coconuts at the weekend. He's the shy and retiring type.

I saw Lionel Richie at the circus with a performing cat. I said to myself, 'What a feline, dancing on the ceiling.'

I dumped my Rastafarian boyfriend after he made me eat his hair. The thought of him shoving his long locks down my throat filled me with dread.

I planned to make a yacht out of stone but changed my mind.
It was too much of a hardship.

A multiple-choice teacher was appointed headmistress at my local school.
It appears she ticked all the right boxes.

I burst out crying every time I see a Biro lid.
My doctor asked me: "How long have you had these pen top emotions?"

An Asian crime lord wants to know how he is going to sell all his Chinese gangster paraphernalia.
He said: "I might triads."

I went to my doctor with stomach pains after eating a small wading bird.
He told me I had a coot appendicitis.

My friend keeps bowing to pressure to wear a size 6 dress.
I don't think she should. She's bigger than that.

There's been a government crackdown on faulty fertility clocks.
New legislation will mean women should buy a logical clock.

I was arrested for planting a giant Redwood on the grounds of Buckingham Palace.
They said I am to be charged with high treeson.

I was distraught after missing my therapy session for self-harming.
My friend said: "Don't beat yourself up about it."

I wanted to murder my neighbour by hitting him with the neck of my guitar.
It's not the first time I've made a death fret like this.

I went to a fancy-dress party as an alarm clock.
I left early because everybody was winding me up.

U2 singer, Bono, is in a critical condition after falling off a stage.
He was too close to The Edge.

I collapsed in a curry house after
hearing rock band REM have
split up.
That's me in the korma.

A man has died after falling into a
giant coffee vat.
He didn't suffer. It was instant.

A killer has used sandpaper to
murder his victim.
He told police he only meant to
rough him up.

Sophie Ellis Bexter arrested after the murder of a football legend.
It was murder on Zidane's floor.

A man was seen out with a Blackpool MP. She looked like a stick of rock.
A lovely candy date.

My silly mate wanted to drive back to his house, drunk.
I told him he could crash at mine.

My deaf ex-girlfriend cheated on
me with another deaf guy.
I should have seen the signs.

An astrologer was asked if he
knew anything about the absence
of Halley's flaming meteorite.
No comet.

Wrestling organisers plan to
hold a sumo competition near a
Buddhist monastery.
Fat chants!

I am desperate to sell my Adam & The Ants book collection at a reduced price.
I'll even throw in a stand and deliver.

I do public relations for a company that sells bicycle wheels.
I am their spokesperson.

I'm concerned for my friend, who puts bubble wrap around his wooden shoes.
I'm worried he might pop his clogs.

A man has died after falling down
a steaming hot power plant.
He will be mist.

Nutritionists have warned against
eating wooden shoes from
Holland.
It appears they clog up the
digestive system.

I bought my girlfriend an e-book
reader.
I thought it would rekindle our
relationship.

'Batman' shampoo is now available in your local supermarket.
Hopefully, they will soon be selling conditioner Gordon.

Someone has stolen all my vintage vinyl LPs.
Police say they are looking for Prince.

I broke my neck when I fell into purple shrubs.
I'll have to be more careful in fuchsia.

A fisherman keeps getting angry
every time his boat drifts off.
I think he needs anchor
management.

ALL dogs are only good for
cleaning floors!
That's a sweeping general alsatian.

My friend started a new business
selling oversized bathroom
equipment.
He asked me to give him a massive
plug.

I dreamt I was drowning in vodka.
It was an Absolut nightmare.

I painted my old clothes stand.
I'll give it another coat tomorrow.

I watched a horror film, set in
Russia, about politicians who
turned into savages when fed after
midnight.
Kremlins.

An Asian man complained of long shifts through the Chinese New Year.
He said the days were dragon in.

A boy told his grandmother she had bad posture.
She got the hump.

Music composer was criticised for insisting his chauffeur plays his classical music CD in the car.
He's always been a Bach seat driver.

I was astounded when I saw a vegetable being delivered to my local library. I thought that was a turnip for the books.

My budgie has escaped from its cage and humped the family dog. Now I have puppies going cheep if anyone wants one.

I am worried about head lice in my eyebrows.
My friend said: "Don't worry, they are just out on the lash."

Two arsonists fall in love.
They are getting on like a house on fire.

I was thinking of getting a sculpture of my face, but I shouldn't get a head of myself.

A police officer was embarrassed when the toilet wouldn't flush after he took a crap.
He said: "I've completely lost faith in the cistern."

The venue for my therapy session changed to a monastery.
I found it hard to talk at first, but then I realised we were a monk's friends.

My TV set keeps winking at me.
I think it's on the blink.

A panto star who plays a giant told me about an obsessed fan.
He said: "It seems she's beanstalking me."

I think my dentist is a bit of a Nazi, but he told me: "That couldn't be Führer from the tooth."

When I ate at my local Chinese restaurant, I ordered from 'The Specials' menu.
I think I had 'Too Much Foo Young'.

I tried to finish my jigsaw puzzle but accidentally swallowed a part of it.
I'm now trying to find my inner-peace.

I never realized I was addicted to
crossword puzzles.
Now when I look back, all the
clues were there.

I keep having dreams about a
horse in full battle.
When I think about it, it's probably
a knight mare.

I struggled with my pregnancy.
Nine months doesn't seem that
long, but to me, it was like a
maternity.

I struggled to sleep, so I went to my doctors. He suggested sleeping on the edge of the bed.
I'd soon drop off.

My New Year's resolution is to be a bit more patient.
I hope to accomplish this as fast as possible.

An unemployed man was offered a job as an undertaker.
He told friends he just couldn't dig it.

My wife couldn't accept my addiction to horoscopes.
In the end, it Taurus apart.

NASA and Star Wars collaborate to build a robot that can change direction in space.
'R2 Detour' is expected to be launched next year.

A Scottish biscuit factory is to close just before New Year.
Bosses say they won't be able to produce shortbread any longer.

Scientists got bored watching the
Earth turn for 24-hours.
They decided to call it a day.

An X-ray revealed my pet dog
swallowed a sofa cushion. The
vet described his condition as
'comfortable'.

I let my dolphin go after it was
found to be useless.
It was no longer fit for porpoise.

I was admitted to a library instead of a hospital.
I had to suffer in silence.

New Adam Ant diet is taking the world by storm.
'Don't Chew Ever, Don't Chew Ever'.

Office worker announces she will give up using spreadsheets for 40-days and 40-nights. Her boss reckons she will be Excel Lent.

Pop diva, Mariah Carey, was given a piece of residential land for her services to the music industry.
She said she didn't want a lot for Christmas.

A man bought a wig before going on holiday.
His friend gave him a comb as a parting gift.

Housewife grew tired of all her laundry duties.
She eventually threw in the towel.

I turned down a job working in the fruit market.
They wanted to pay me in vegetables, but the celery was unacceptable.

I received a tiny globe as a gift from an old friend I haven't seen in years.
It's a small world.

Tributes pour in for skydiver after his parachute failed to open.
His friends said he was down to earth.

A teenager locked herself in her room in a bid to cure her acne. She still hasn't broken out yet.

A bomb was thrown into the kitchen of a leading French statesman.
Linoleum Blownapart.

I was attacked by a gang of yobs who beat me with calendars. It looked like my days were numbered.

Woman kidnapped by mime artists claims they did unspeakable things to her.

Donald Trump has banned sliced cheese in a bid to make America grate again.

I entered an astrology competition in my local newspaper.
I didn't win, but they sent me a map of the stars as a constellation prize.

My friend, who works as a chef in a tapas bar, refused to reveal his recipe for fajitas.
He said he was keeping it under wraps.

I injured myself, tripping over a drum kit.
I had percussion.

Our local fisherman used liquorice as bait.
He claims he has caught Allsorts.

I got fired from my job at the Pepsi factory.
I tested positive for Coke.

A boiled egg every morning is hard to beat.

I knew my girlfriend was a ghost after she walked through the door.

Minnie saves Mickey from drowning in Disney horror.
She gave him mouse-to-mouse resuscitation.

I was in the market for a new
chicken coop.
I told potential sellers it must be
impeccable.

I thought my wife was joking after
she threatened to leave me because
I kept singing 'I'm a believer', but
then I saw her face.

I had to go to a Whitesnake
concert alone after my mates
pulled out.
I thought, 'Here I go again, on my
own'.

My best friend joined a cult that worships black holes.
I'd hate to get sucked into something like that.

A filmmaker working on a new movie about broken bones is currently looking for a cast.

My neighbour played the same Lionel Richie song on repeat.
I wouldn't mind, but it was all night long.

Fishermen who like to take risks are accused of pushing the boat out.

Kylie Minogue opened her own kebab takeaway.
Her friend said she's come a long way since selling from 'Jason's Doner Van'.

Voters struggle to get aroused by any political party.
They suffer from electile dysfunction.

My wife can't stop singing Tom Jones' 'Delilah'. She asked her doctor if it was common.
He said it's not unusual.

I bet my husband he could never build a car out of spaghetti.
He told his friends: "You should have seen her face as I drove pasta."

I was being followed by a giant bird.
I think I was being storked.

I told my wife it was her turn to
put salt on the front steps.
All I got was icy stares.

I bought the new '007 Viagra'.
It makes you roger more.

I was thrown out of a casino
following an altercation with a
croupier.
It seems she had a chip on her
shoulder.

I was diagnosed with budgie flu.
My doctor said it was tweetable.

I had to close my origami business.
It folded.

If we got rid of margarine and
spreads, the world would be a
butter place.

A whistleblower exposed a
corrupt coffin business.
He threatened to lift the lid.

Did you hear about the great duct
tape heist?
I have no idea how they pulled
that off.

A thief stole my thesaurus.
I am lost for words.

My local bar was full of people
covered in rashes.
It must have been shingles night.

My mum hesitates when ordering
something at her local restaurant.
I think she's going through the
menu-pause.

I tried to kill myself by going
down a shoot and into a drain.
It was a sewer slide attempt.

Donkey forced to walk a tightrope.
My ass is on the line.

I failed my italic writing exam.
I got straight As.

I spent £100 pounds on a belt that doesn't fit.
It was a huge waist.

I auditioned for a part in a bread commercial.
The director said I was perfect for that roll.

My recipe business 'Cooking With Herbs' has gone burst.
The bank has called in the bay leafs.

I watched a documentary about beavers.
It was the best dam documentary I've ever seen.

Did you hear about the 2ft
ballerina covered in ink.
The girl with the dragging tutu.

Skyscraper splits in half.
There are always two sides to
every storey.

Snow White turned away from
Photo Express.
She said: "I'm sick and tired of
waiting on my prints."

I am convinced my eyes and skin
are changing colour.
I've been told it's a pigment of my
imagination.

Drones for sale.
We expect them to fly off the
shelves.

I downloaded the film Titanic onto
my iPad.
It's synching now.

Argos has a half-price offer on
trampolines.
I expect people will jump on it.

I thought I had a dream about
a Chinese man, but I made a
mistake, it was just my imagine
Asian.

A poker player was upset after
losing his arm.
He had to get a prosthetic one and
had a hard time dealing with it.

I went to a private investigator with a pencil and a sheet of paper and asked him to trace someone for me.

A nun asked to borrow some black and white fabric.
I told her: "Just don't make a habit out of it."

My son is critical after falling off a trampoline.
I hope he will bounce back.

I tried to call the ladder store
today but couldn't get through.
It just rung and rung.

My friend writes lyrics about
sewing machines.
She's a Singer-songwriter.

Museum curators are furious
about having to work after dark
moving suits of armour.
It seems they hate knight shifts.

My friend has OCD and arranges her dinner plates by the year they were bought.
It's an extremely rare dish order.

A man who has wrinkled clothing is diagnosed with an iron deficiency.

I was relieved when I got my upper torso waxed.
It was great to get it all off my chest.

My coffee cup was stolen.
I now have to go down the police
station and look at mugshots.

I keep taking photos of myself
beside boiling kettles.
I think I have selfie steam issues.

I regret enrolling in an engraving
workshop.
There's so much to learn; I've
barely scratched the surface.

A scuba diver instructor quit his job.
He said: "Deep down, it wasn't for me."

Pop group 'Skinny Jeans' stormed the charts.
I had a listen, but I couldn't really get into them.

I owned a horse that only stayed awake when it was dark.
It was a night mare.

I live by the coast and consult the tide charts every day.
I like to keep up with current events.

I am suspicious of my friend who buys smoke machines.
I think he is part of an extreme mist group.

I want to buy a yacht, but they are too expensive. I think I'll wait for the sails.

I want to learn how to play golf, but I still have a fairway to go.

Yorkshire police have said all their satnavs were stolen. They are still searching for Leeds.

I got sacked from my job making rucksacks.
I plan to sue the company for back pay.

My local sauna has closed down.
It ran out of steam.

Thieves have made off with a
cement mixer.
Police are looking for concrete
evidence.

My doctor claims he's never made
a joke about an unvaccinated baby.
He said: "I'll give it a shot."

There was a robbery at the adhesive factory.
Police are unable to tape off the area.

The Pope lashes out at non-believers and atheists.
He said: "If you don't believe Jesus rose from the dead, then you have ascension deficit disorder.

A man in our pub claims he bumped into Lancelot in the toilets holding a luminous pen.
He said it was the highlight of the knight.

I saw a group of men wearing nun's habits and earphones, dancing to crazy music.
I think it was Monastery of Sound.

A debate on whether to bring back hanging continues.
A judge said: "It's a good idea if executed properly."

A serial killer was slammed for collecting body parts in India.
He claimed he was given the Goa head.

My son's maths teacher was caught with a large collection of graph paper and pencils.
I think he's plotting something.

My friend tried to set me up with an American rodent.
He's not the type I'd typically gopher.

Apparently, a maniac went on a rampage in our local town, attacking everyone with a sharp pencil.
Police say the details are a bit sketchy.

My wife attacked me with a builder's spirit level in a bid to get even.

Rare and valuable dog stolen. Police say they have a lead.

Dentists to go on strike. Patients urged to brace themselves.

Scandinavian air hostess missing.
Police say she disappeared into
Finnair.

I once dressed as sliced bread at a
fancy-dress party.
You should have seen the birds;
they were all over me.

The local kleptomaniacs meeting
was packed out.
All the seats were taken.

The inventor of the hard-boiled
egg has died.
RIP Scott Chegg.

I had a nightmare about German
sausages invading the country.
I feared the würst.

Farmer arrested for stealing giant
haystacks.
He was let out on bale.

Police warn the public not to phone a scam amputee helpline. You might get cut off.

Donald Trump sentenced to hanging in an impeachment trial. His lawyer said: "He's asked for fake noose."

The escalators came to a halt in the shopping mall.
Everyone just stopped and staired.

A woman's suspenders were stolen from the washing line. Neighbours say she's not holding up well.

There was a massive flood in the lemonade factory. 500 staff were Schwepped away.

There was a huge fire at the shoe factory. Reports confirm 1000 soles lost.

Dalai Lama confesses to a
gambling habit.
He likes Tibet.

Thief on the run after stealing
pants in order of size.
Police say he's still at large.

Haemorrhoids leaflets were stolen
from our local clinic.
The doctor told staff not to worry
as he has piles.

Rumours of butter factory closure spread quickly throughout the town.

Explosion in French cheese factory.
Reports say there's nothing left but de Brie.

U2 have started using razor blades instead of plectrums.
It's cutting Edge.

Bonnie Tyler released a video
about cardiology.
It's totally clips of the heart.

Gerry Rafferty once owned a
ladies' boutique.
Gowns to the left of me, chokers to
the right.

Pop band a-ha lose phone battery
charger on their tour bus.
They've been hunting high and
low.

Elvis returned shoes to sender after discovering they were made in China.
He was looking for a little less Converse Asian.

Poet Rabbie Burns was accused of stealing a kilt.
He plaid guilty.

Lonely tennis player complains she can't find happiness in a relationship.
Love means nothing to her.

Paranoid rugby player quits club. Every time there was a scrum, he thought everyone was talking about him.

Woman with the world's first glass diaphragm says: "Now I have a womb with a view."

Aftershave sales have slumped. People are just not splashing out these days.

I quit the quicksand business.
I was up to my neck in it.

I bought a property in France
even although I was a little cash
strapped.
I had nothing Toulouse.

Private photos of Bugs Bunny have
been released.
You can see them on WhatsApp
doc.

A nurse complained she was verbally abused while treating a patient.
She said: "He was adding insult to injury."

I only have one leg and work at the local brewery.
They put me in charge of the hops.

My paranoid friend quit working as a taxi driver.
He said he was sick of passengers talking behind his back.

Our local farmer grazed his cows in cannabis fields.
The pot roasts are amazing.

I was gravely injured changing a wheel after some idiot kicked the jack away. I wish I knew who it was.
The suspension is killing me.

My new girlfriend gave me a sexually transmitted disease.
I'm now gonorrhoea-valuate our relationship.

I bought a book on how to survive
falling down the stairs.
It's a step-by-step guide.

I attended a Scottish military
wedding where the bride received
two black eyes.
Guests blamed the 'Bashing White
Sergeant'.

I was asked on a date by a woman
with a really loud voice.
I had to turn her down.

My wife ended up in therapy due to her addiction to crosswords.
I hope she doesn't feel two down.

I had to quit my job at the cat shelter.
They reduced meowers.

A man in a wheelchair stole a camouflage jacket from a store.
The manager told him: "You can hide, but you cannot run."

My wife has this weird phobia
about speed bumps.
She's slowly getting over it now.

Some sock puppets were stolen
from the local theatre for the third
time this week.
Police say it's getting out of hand.

My plumber boyfriend avoids
paying tax by installing long metal
rods down toilets.
He says it's a loo pole.

I ended my relationship with a
blow-up doll.
I let her down gently.

My girlfriend insists I tell her the
time right down to the nearest
60th of a minute.
I think she's just using me for secs.

A dominatrix business was saved
from the brink of collapse.
Customers had a whip-round.

A woman who claims to have had regular sex with a ghost was accused of having a phantom pregnancy.

My grandfather survived pepper spray and mustard gas during the war.
He's a seasoned veteran.

A man with a stammer was jailed. The judge rules he's unlikely to complete his sentence.

If you never played darts
blindfolded, you don't know what
you're missing.

My next-door neighbour died after
overdosing on Viagra.
His wife took it hard.

Government issues call to be more
respectful to blind prostitutes.
You've got to hand it to them.

My work colleague was arrested for dressing up like a deck of cards.
Police say the judge will deal with him accordingly.

I lost my job as a fish filleter.
I was gutted.

I had to drop leaflets through doors on the causes of flatulence.
Unfortunately, I let one rip.

I dumped my chauffeur boyfriend.
It felt like he was always driving
me away.

My daughter went upstairs to get
some medicine
I think she's coming down with
something.

My mate fears he will lose his job
at the printers where they produce
calendars.
He took a day off, and now he
thinks his days are numbered.

Voodoo dolls were stolen from an African store.
Police are trying to pin down the suspects.

My husband was warned about his sodium consumption before he died.
He took the doctor's advice with a pinch of salt.

My Weight Watchers class has been cancelled.
It's all gone belly up.

Cruise line companies are going bust.
They've been forced to look for new horizons.

Andrex is the latest company to hit the skids.
A spokesperson for the toilet tissue company said: "Business has gone down the pan."

My neighbour keeps shouting: 'Castles!' 'Ramparts!' and 'Drawbridge!'
I think he has turrets syndrome.

I foolishly booked a holiday to
view the horizon.
I can see it far enough.

I once swallowed a comic book.
It gave me a belly full of laughs.

I heard Meatloaf married his
accountant girlfriend.
She will do anything for love, but
she won't do VAT.

A publication by Plan4 Media
in association with Daily Dafty

For more information, please visit:
plan4media.com
dailydafty.com

9 781907 463877